Savvy

Girlology

BODY PRO

Facts and Figures About Bad Hair Days, Blemishes, and Being Healthy

by Erin Falligant

CAPSTONE PRESS
a capstone imprint

Savvy Books are published by Capstone Press,
1710 Roe Crest Drive, North Mankato, Minnesota 56003
www.mycapstone.com

Library of Congress Cataloging-in-Publication Data
Names: Falligant, Erin, author.
Title: Body pro : facts and figures about bad hair days, blemishes and being healthy / by Erin Falligant.
Description: North Mankato, Minnesota : an imprint of Capstone Press, [2018]
  | Series: Savvy. Girlology | Audience: Ages 9-13.
Identifiers: LCCN 2017046820 (print) | LCCN 2017047311 (ebook) |
ISBN 9781515778820 (ebook PDF) | ISBN 9781515778783 (hardcover)
Subjects: LCSH: Girls—Health and hygiene—Juvenile literature. | Grooming
  for girls—Juvenile literature.
Classification: LCC RA777.25 (ebook) | LCC RA777.25 .F35 2018 (print) | DDC
  646.7/046—dc23
LC record available at https://lccn.loc.gov/2017046820

Editorial Credits
Mandy Robbins, editor; Kayla Rossow, designer; Jo Miller, media researcher;
Kathy McColley, production specialist

Photo Credits
Getty Images: Hulton Archive/Stringer, 19bl, Shutterstock: aarrows, 30bl, Africa Studio, 25bl, Akkalak Aiempradit, 11tr, Aleks Melnik, 29b, 35bl, 35br, amelissimo, 24r, Anastacia Trapeznikova, 24l, Anastasiia Skorobogatova, 25ml, AnaV, 13bl, Andrey_Popov, 39m, Andy Dean Photography, 31r, Ann Haritonenko, 31ml, Annie Dove, 24l, asantosg, 15r, asharkyu, 11mr, AYakovlev, 37tl, bigacis, 25tm, Binh Thanh Bui, 23tm, 23tr, borsvelka, 24l, Brainsil, 10, Bryan Solomon, 7, Catherine Glazkova, 43bm, Chones, 40, chronicler, 24r, curiosity, 24l, designer_an, 47t, Designua, 12b, Diana Taliun, 23br, Eugene Onischenko, 37tm, Evikka, 25tr, Fatseyeva, 29tr, Flaffy, 25m, flowerstock, 14tr, Gelpi, 35t, Gino Santa Maria, 37tr, GMEVIPHOTO, 28tr, Hong Vo, 28tl, ImageFlow, 44, iordani, 46, Iraida-art, 34, , 35r, jamie cross, 28b, Jane_Lane, 43br, JeniFoto, 25br, jocic, 39l, Left, Josep Curto, 23bl, Julia Moskalenko, 14bl, Kamieshkova, 24r, KeKi Chulaket, 11b, Kencana Studio, 24tr, KucherAV, 25tl, Lermot, 24r, little_one, 14tl, LynxVector, 18, M. Unal Ozmen, 29bl, 29mr, 39ml, MaeManee, 45, magicoven, 39r, MANDY GODBEHEAR, 4, MaraZe, 23bm, Marushchak Olha, 30t, mhatzapa, 24r, Michal Sanca, 30br, Monkey Business Images, 33b, Moving Moment, 29br, nikiteev_ konstantin, 20, Nitr, 39mr, Middle Oleg GawriloFF, 41, Olga_Angelloz, 47b, OzonE_AnnA, 37b, pathdoc, 21, paulista, 29ml, Photo Melon, 17t, pukach, 13br, Rawpixel.com, 16, Rohappy, 31l, Romariolen, 25bm, Samuel Borges Photography, 31m, schiva, 14br, shekaka, 33m, Skobrik, 19tr, Sonya illustration, 12t, stereoliar, 5, 13tl, swinner, 25mr, Syda Productions, 42, Syrytsyna Tetiana, 43t, szefei, 31mr, Tania Khalaziy, 33t, Tatiana Ka, 43bl, Tim UR, 23tl, Vangelis Vassalakis, 29t, VGstockstudio, 32, Vixit, 24r, Vladimir Gjorgiev, 9tl, wavebreakmedia, 22, xxllxx, 15l

Design Elements
Capstone Studio: Karon Dubke; Shutterstock: AD Hunter, Atlantis Images, Alena Ohneva, Alsou Shakurova, Angie Makes, Antun Hirsman, AnyRama, Brian Chase, Dzha33, graphixmania, Icons vector, krasivo, Macrovector, Mariam27, MicroOne, Pavel K, Pushistaja, RomanYa, vavavka, Yulia Yemelianova

Printed and bound in the USA.
010846S18

TABLE OF CONTENTS

Chapter 1

KNOW YOUR BODY

How fast do your hair and nails grow? What percentage of girls struggle with pimples? How much sleep do you *really* need at night? Get the facts and figures about your body, and learn how other girls view and care for themselves too. Knowing the numbers can help you feel more confident about your growing, changing body. It will also help you know what to expect *next*.

age 8:
Most girls begin puberty between the ages of 8 and 13.

age 9:
50% of girls ages 9 to 12 think they're overweight, but only 15% actually are.

age 10:
The average girl begins her growth spurt at age 10. Girls can grow 3.5 inches (9 centimeters) per year during puberty.

age 11:
76% of 11-year-olds do NOT get enough exercise each day.

The average girl gets her first bra at age 11½.

age 12:
71% of parents think it's okay for a 12-year-old girl to begin shaving her legs.

The average girl gets her period at age 12.

age 13:
71% of 13-year-olds do NOT get enough sleep on school nights.

50% of girls wear makeup between the ages of 11 and 13 years old.

age 14:
15% of 14- to 17-year-olds wear contacts.

An active 14-year-old needs 2400 calories a day.

HAIR, HERE AND THERE

You cut it, you clip it, you brush it, and you braid it. When hair starts to grow in new places, you might even pluck and shave it. Get all the hairy details here.

100,000:
approximate number of hairs on your head

2 to 6:
how many years each hair "lives" on your head

50 to 100:
strands that fall out each day

0.04 to 0.1 millimeter:
the thickness of a strand of hair

1/2 inch:
your hair's average growth each month

5 feet:
how long your hair could grow if you never cut it

HOW OFTEN SHOULD YOU SHAMPOO?
Shampooing too often can dry out your hair and scalp. How often is enough for you? Answer these questions to find out.

Want to shower on non-shampoo days?
Just rinse your hair with water and use conditioner.
Presto – healthier hair!

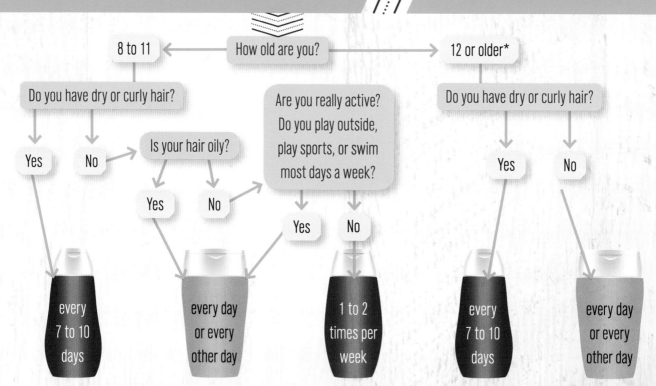

How old are you?

8 to 11
- Do you have dry or curly hair?
  - Yes → every 7 to 10 days
  - No → Is your hair oily?
    - Yes → every day or every other day
    - No → Are you really active? Do you play outside, play sports, or swim most days a week?
      - Yes → every day or every other day
      - No → 1 to 2 times per week

12 or older*
- Do you have dry or curly hair?
  - Yes → every 7 to 10 days
  - No → every day or every other day

*If you're not quite 12 but have started puberty, follow the tips for ages 12 and older.

HAIR ON LEGS AND UNDERARMS

Puberty may cause the hair on your legs to get darker and thicker. You'll grow hair under your arms too. Some girls and women choose to shave it. Others leave it. Talk to your parents and decide what's right for you.

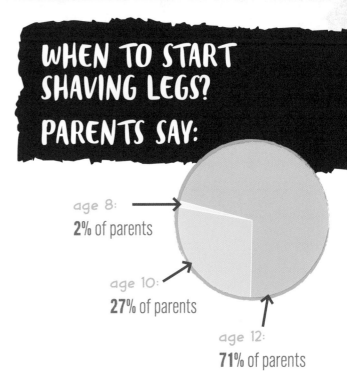

WHEN TO START SHAVING LEGS? PARENTS SAY:

age 8: **2%** of parents

age 10: **27%** of parents

age 12: **71%** of parents

FACIAL HAIR

Some girls worry about thick eyebrows or the darkening of hair above their upper lip. Shaving isn't usually the best removal option for facial hair. When you shave off the soft tip, hair can feel coarse as it grows back. Tweezing and waxing, which remove hair at the root, last longer.

INGROWN HAIR

An ingrown hair is one that curls around and grows back into your skin. It can cause an itchy or painful red bump. Shaving, waxing, and tweezing can all cause ingrown hairs. Follow a parent or guardian's advice for the safest way to remove hair.

How Often You Need To:							
tweeze	3 to 8 weeks						
wax	3 to 6 weeks						
shave	1 to 3 days						
week	1	2	3	4	5	6	7	8

THE DOWNSIDES?

Tweezing and waxing can be painful and expensive. Most parents want girls to wait until they're at least 14.

When is it okay for girls to start tweezing or waxing?

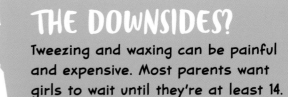

age **16**: 32% of parents

age **14**: 30% of parents

age **12**: 19% of parents

HANDS AND NAILS

Your hands and nails say a lot about you. But it takes time to care for them — and to break that pesky nail-biting habit.

SUDS UP

Handwashing is the most important way to prevent spreading germs, illness, and infection. But only . . .

58% of teen girls and 48% of teen boys wash their hands after using the restroom.

Kids who wash their hands at least 4 times a day take . . .

51% fewer sick days due to stomach illness.

24% fewer sick days from school due to colds and the flu.

20 seconds: the amount of time you should spend washing your hands to make sure they're really clean

GROWING YOUR NAILS

Fingernails grow faster than toenails, especially on your dominant hand. If you're right handed, the nails on your right hand grow faster! And all nails grow faster in the summer than in the winter.

3.5: how many millimeters fingernails grow each month (That's 1/8 of an inch.)

1: the number of millimeters toenails grow each month

6: the number of months it might take to grow back a fingernail if you lost one in an injury

18: how many months it might take to grow back a lost toenail

HEALTHY NAILS = HEALTHY BODY

Changes in your nails could be a sign of other health problems. Tell your parents or your doctor if:

- you notice a dark streak under a nail.
- your nails' natural color changes.
- your nails get thicker or thinner.
- the skin swells around a nail.

NAIL NIBBLERS

50% of kids between ages 10 and 18 bite their nails.

30 is the age when most people outgrow the habit.

TO PAINT OR NOT TO PAINT?

Nail polish and polish remover can be hard on your nails.

3 the number of chemicals that make up the "toxic trio" in many nail polishes

The toxic trio:
- Formaldehyde—can cause cancer.
- Toluene—can cause dizziness, nausea, headaches, and eye problems.
- Dibutyl phthalate (DBP)—can cause reproductive problems.

If you polish your nails, do it in a well-ventilated space. Look for water-based polishes. And choose a moisturizing polish remover or one without acetone, a chemical that dries out nails.

10 out of 12 nail polishes labeled as being "toxin free" actually contain toxic chemicals.

EYES, EARS, AND MOUTH

Are you getting contacts? Already wearing braces?
Thinking about piercing your ears? You're not alone!

CHANGING EYES

As you get older, chances
are greater that you'll need a
prescription to correct your
vision. One study showed
that nearly a third of teens
wear glasses or contacts.

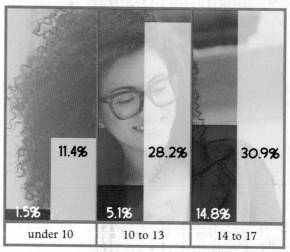

contact lenses

prescription eyeglasses

	11.4%	28.2%	30.9%
1.5%		5.1%	14.8%
under 10	10 to 13	14 to 17

WANT TO TRY CONTACTS?

30 MILLION
people in the U.S.
wear contact lenses.

12 or 13
is how old most
experts think kids
should be before
they get contacts.

5%
of people under 18
wear contact lenses.
(That's **3.9 million**
kids and teens.)

WHY WAIT? BECAUSE ...

• **68%** of contact lens wearers
don't correctly follow the care
instructions given to them.

• About **25%** of children's
emergency room visits each year
have to do with eye infections or
injuries caused by contacts.

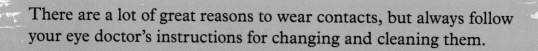

There are a lot of great reasons to wear contacts, but always follow
your eye doctor's instructions for changing and cleaning them.

PIERCED EARS

Did you know that about 83% of American men and women have their earlobes pierced? If you have pierced ears or are thinking of getting them pierced, you need to know how to care for them properly.

CARING FOR PIERCED EARS

1 how many times a day you should wash your pierced ears with soap and water

2 how many times a day you should apply alcohol with a cotton ball

3 how many times a day you should gently twist the studs in your ears

6 the number of weeks you should leave studs in, even at night, until your ears are completely healed

Note: If your ears feel sore, look red or puffy, or ooze liquid, have your doctor check them for infection.

BRACES

Getting braces? Join the club!

- **5.75 million** people get orthodontic treatment every year in the U.S. and Canada
- **9 to 14:** the age range when most kids get braces
- **2 years:** the average length of time braces are worn
- **3 tips for surviving braces:**
  - Brush teeth after every snack or meal.
  - Floss every night. Ask your orthodontist to show you tricks for getting above brackets.
  - Steer clear of hard foods or sticky foods that can break or loosen braces.

SKIN SMARTS

Struggling with acne? Experimenting with makeup? Many other girls are too. Here are some stats on the skin you're in.

ABOUT ACNE

8 in 10
tweens and teens
have acne.

17 million
people in the U.S.
have acne.

1 to 2:
how many times
you should wash
your face each day

3 Fictions:
- Chocolate causes acne.
  (It doesn't.)
- Greasy foods cause acne.
  (They don't.)
- Stress causes acne.
  (It doesn't either.)

3 Facts:
- Changes in hormones during
  puberty can cause acne.
- Acne may be hereditary.
  (If your parents had acne,
  you might too.)
- Greasy makeup can lead to acne.
  Always wash it off at night
  with a gentle cleanser.

HOW ACNE DEVELOPS

A pimple forms when a healthy pore becomes a clogged pore. Bacteria spreads within the gland beneath the skin.

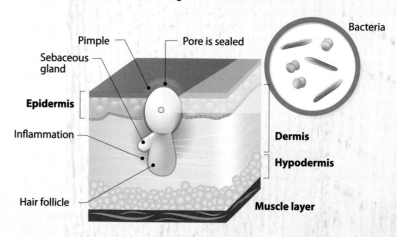

- Pimple
- Pore is sealed
- Bacteria
- Sebaceous gland
- **Epidermis**
- Inflammation
- **Dermis**
- **Hypodermis**
- Hair follicle
- **Muscle layer**

MAKEUP? MAYBE, MAYBE NOT

3 out of 5 girls
ages 8 to 18 wear makeup.

WHEN DID THEY START?

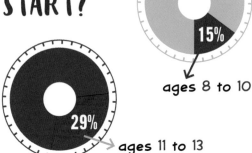

15%
ages 8 to 10

29%
ages 11 to 13

ages 14 to 16
50%

TOP MAKEUP PICKS FOR TWEENS?

15% wear eyeliner.

15% wear lipstick.

18% wear mascara.

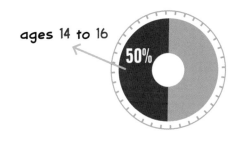

OF THE GIRLS WHO WEAR MAKEUP . . .

- **80%** feel fine about themselves when they don't wear it, and . . .
- **73%** feel fine leaving the house without it.
- **5%** say going without makeup makes them feel more attractive.

2/27/12:

The date when the first Barefaced & Beautiful, Within and Without campaign kicked off. It encouraged girls and women to go without makeup for a day — and to post selfies on social media. Barefaced can be beautiful!

Celebrities such as Alicia Keys and Alessia Cara have embraced a makeup-free lifestyle. Many of their fans have done the same.

SUN STATS AND TANNING TRUTHS

Tanning damages your skin — it's that simple. There's no such thing as a safe tan, and no skin tone that's safe from skin cancer. So before you have fun in the sun, know the numbers — and protect yourself.

ON SPF

SPF (Sun Protection Factor) measures how well a sunscreen protects your skin. As the SPF goes up, so does the percentage of UVB rays the sunscreen filters out. But doubling the SPF doesn't double your protection, and no sunscreen can block 100 percent of the sun's rays. See for yourself:

SPF 8: **87%** of UVB rays

SPF 15: **93%** of UVB rays

SPF 30: **97%** of UVB rays

SPF 50: **98%** of UVB rays

SPF 100: **99%** of UVB rays

10 a.m. to 2 p.m. is when the sun is highest in the sky. Seek shade or slather on sunscreen during the sun's strongest hours!

80% of the sun's rays can penetrate skin even on cloudy days.

30 is the lowest SPF you should wear when heading outside. Choose one with broad-spectrum protection. It protects against both types of sunlight that can damage skin, known as UVA and UVB rays.

30 is also the SPF protection your lips need. Look for lip balm with sunscreen in it.

HEADING TO THE BEACH?

15 — 15 minutes before you leave: apply sunscreen. It takes time to absorb into your skin.

¼ to ½ — ¼ to ½ ounce is how much most people actually use.

2 — Every 2 hours you should reapply sunscreen if you're out of the water.

1 — 1 ounce is the amount of sunscreen dermatologists say you should use.

80 — Every 80 minutes is how often you should reapply water-resistant sunscreen if you're swimming.

THE TRUTH ABOUT TANNING

Think tanning indoors (using a tanning bed, booth, or lamp) is safer for your skin than spending time in the sun? Think again!

1 in 10 high school girls have tried a tanning device.

56% of teens who tan say they've gotten a burn from a tanning device.

400,000 skin cancer cases each year are caused by indoor tanning.

59%: your increased risk for melanoma, the deadliest kind of skin cancer, if you tan indoors before age 35

18: the age you now have to be in the following states before you're allowed to tan indoors: California, Delaware, Hawaii, Illinois, Kansas, Louisiana, Massachusetts, Minnesota, Nevada, New Hampshire, North Carolina, Oregon, Texas, Vermont, and Washington

Chapter 2
GROWING, GROWING, GROWN

Puberty is all about growth. Maybe you already hit your growth spurt and sailed past the boys in your class. But they'll catch up! Girls and boys hit their growth spurts at different ages, and everyone grows at his or her own rate.

2.5 inches: average child's growth per year between age 2 and the start of puberty

3.5 inches: average girl's growth per year during puberty

9 to 11: when most girls begin their growth spurt

15 to 18: when most girls reach their full height

13 to 14: the age when most boys begin their growth spurt

20 to 21: when most boys finish growing

GIRLS VS. BOYS

Here's what the average girl's growth spurt looks like next to the average boy's.

| 12 years | 14 years | 16 years | 12 years | 14 years | 16 years | 18 years |

Average height range for girls

Average height range for boys

BREASTS AND BRAS

Like the rest of your body during puberty, breasts grow too. Some girls fear their breasts are growing too quickly. Others fear they're not growing quickly enough. Breast development takes time. In the meantime, find a bra that fits.

10

10 to 11:
the age when most girls' breasts begin to develop (But it can start as early as age 7 or as late as age 13.)

11

11 to 12:
the average age when a girl gets her first bra

12

12 to 13:
the average age when a girl gets a bra with a cup size

13

UNEVEN BREASTS?

Breasts often grow at different rates during puberty. The difference in size will even out as you get older. But more than **50%** of adult women have some kind of breast asymmetry. That means their breasts don't match exactly. And it's perfectly normal!

BRA BASICS

cups

bra straps

underwire

bra bands

bra hooks

Don't know what size you wear? Do the math:

1. Use a tape measure to measure your rib cage, just under your breasts.

2. Add 5 inches.

3. Did you get an odd number (such as 29, 31, or 33)? If so, subtract 1 to round down to the nearest even number (such as 28, 30, or 32), as bras usually stretch over time. The total is your band size.

4. Measure across the fullest part of your breasts. Subtract your band size from this number. The answer to this equation is your cup size:

$$0'' = AA \qquad 1'' = A \qquad 2'' = B$$

$$3'' = C \qquad 4'' = D$$

5. Put your band size together with your cup size to get your bra size (such as 32A).

8 out of 10 women wear bras that don't fit!

Need help? Ask for it! An older sister, your mom or aunt, or even a salesperson at a department store can help you find your best fit.

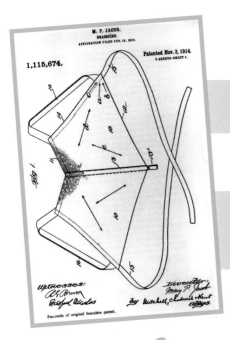

Facsimile of original brassière patent.

THE FIRST BRA—EVER!

1914: when the first modern bra was invented

19: Mary Phelps Jacob's age when she invented the bra

2: the number of handkerchiefs she sewed together to create the bra

THE FACTS. PERIOD.

Getting your period can be one of the most exciting — and scariest — parts of puberty. But the more you know ahead of time, the less scary it'll be. Your body already knows what to do, and most likely every woman you know has gone through it.

12
the average age when a girl gets her period (But it can start as early as **8** or as late as **15**.)

2 to 2½ years
how long it often takes to start your period after your breasts start developing

2 tablespoons
the average amount of blood lost during menstruation

Sun	Mon	Tue	Wed	Thu	Fri	Sat
				1	2	3
4	5	6	7	8	9	10
11	12	13	14	15	16	17
18	19	20	21	22	23	24
25	26	27	28	29	30	31

days

2 to 7 days
the length of a normal period

average number of days from the start of your period to the start of your next one. Menstrual cycles can last anywhere from **21 to 45 days**, especially in the first year or two. Track yours on a calendar or with an app, and you'll start to see what's normal for you.

PERIOD MYTHS: TRUE OR FALSE?

1. Period blood differs from the rest of your blood.

2. Certain foods may make cramps worse.

3. You shouldn't exercise during your period.

4. It can take six months or more for a young woman's period to become regular.

✗ 1. FALSE – Blood is the same no matter what part of your body it's from.
✓ 2. TRUE – Avoid the following foods to try to lessen period cramps:
        dairy, sugar, white grains, fatty meat, and salty foods.
✗ 3. FALSE – Exercise may actually boost your mood and lessen cramping.
✓ 4. TRUE – Periods are often irregular the first year a girl has her cycle.

WHAT TO USE?

Some girls use only pads. Other girls use pads when they sleep and tampons during the day. Some prefer menstrual cups. Special absorbent underwear is a new product that may be the right choice for you. Whatever product you use, remember to change it regularly to lower your risk of infection.

Product	Pros	Cons
Pads	-Easy to use -Many options available for coverage and light to heavy flow	-Can be bulky and/or uncomfortable -May leak -May not stay in place while exercising or sleeping
Tampons	-Discreet to carry -No external mess -Able to exercise and swim comfortably	-Can be tricky or intimidating to learn to use -Minor possibility of infection
Menstrual cups	-Can be worn up to 12 hours with no leakage -Reusable cups are environmentally friendly.	-Tricky to learn to use -Reusable cups are messy to clean.
Absorbent underwear	-One pair lasts 25 to 30 washes. -May save you money over time. -Environmentally friendly	-Expensive initial purchase -Washing can be tricky and messy. -You need more than one pair. -May need to be used with a tampon or menstrual cup

Chapter 3

NUTRITION: WHAT YOU MIGHT BE MISSING

To keep your body healthy as it changes and grows, you need to fuel up with the right foods. You know about the major food groups. But do you know if you're getting enough foods from each?

EVERY DAY

Here's how much of each food group experts recommend you eat every day. Take a look at how much girls your age are actually eating.

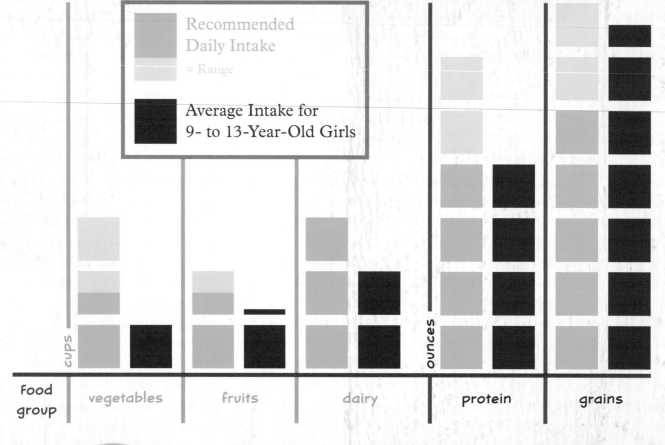

Recommended
Daily Intake
= Range

Average Intake for
9- to 13-Year-Old Girls

cups

ounces

Food group | vegetables | fruits | dairy | protein | grains

WHAT'S A SERVING?

If you're like most girls, you need at least one more serving of fruits and veggies a day — plus another serving of dairy. But what does a "serving" look like?

ONE SERVING

of fruits or veggies looks like this . . .

or this . . .

1 apple

6 baby carrots

or this.

½ cup of broccoli

Need a serving of dairy?

Try this . . .

or this . . .

1 glass of milk

1 container of yogurt

or this.

1 piece of string cheese

Note: Milk and yogurt should be 8-oz. servings.

YOUR BODY ON BREAKFAST

You've heard that it's the most important meal of the day. So why do so many people skip it? You may not be a morning person, but giving yourself time for breakfast will do your body good.

32%

of adolescents don't eat breakfast

10 REASONS NOT TO BAIL ON BREAKFAST

Kids who eat a healthy breakfast may . . .

1. be more punctual

2. miss fewer days of school

3. have a more positive mood

4. pay attention more easily in class

5. find it easier to memorize information

6. get along more easily with peers

7. perform better in math and reading

8. get higher standardized test scores

9. make more nutritious food choices all day long

10. and stay at a healthier weight

. . . than kids who don't.

The best breakfast includes at least 3 out of 5 food groups. Get creative with your combos, even when you're grabbing breakfast on the go.

1 Grain +

1 cup of cooked oatmeal, 1 piece of bread or toast, 1 cup of cereal

1 Fruit or Veggie +

½ apple, a handful of berries, 1 banana

1 Dairy or Protein =

1 tablespoon of peanut butter, 1 container of yogurt, 1 cup of milk

A better breakfast!

SWEET OR SALTY?

Some of us have a sweet tooth. Others go nuts over salty snacks. Whichever you prefer, most of us eat too much sugar and salt. Here are the not-so-sweet facts.

SUGAR

10%
the recommended limit for how many of your daily calories should come from added sugar

17%
the amount that most adolescents ages 9 to 13 actually take in

WHY IT MATTERS

If you're taking in too many calories from sugar, you're probably missing out on the more nutritious foods you need. Plus, too much added sugar can lead to weight gain — and to health problems later on in life.

SUGARY DRINKS

The next time you grab a drink, think. How many spoonfuls of sugar are inside that can or bottle? (Amount in 12-ounce beverages.)

energy drink (10 to 12 tsp)

fruit drink (10 to 11 tsp)

cola (10 tsp)

ginger ale (8 tsp)

sparkling juice or water (7 tsp)

sport drink (5 to 7 tsp)

1% milk (3 tsp)

water (0 tsp)

WHERE DOES ADDED SUGAR COME FROM?

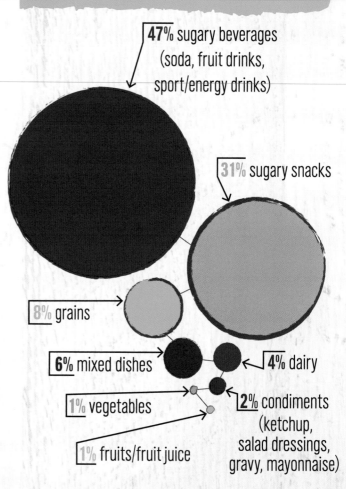

47% sugary beverages (soda, fruit drinks, sport/energy drinks)

31% sugary snacks

8% grains

6% mixed dishes

1% vegetables

1% fruits/fruit juice

4% dairy

2% condiments (ketchup, salad dressings, gravy, mayonnaise)

Not sure how much sugar is inside? Check the label.

SALT

Sure, salty snacks taste great, but salt contains a mineral called sodium that's bad for you in high amounts. Too much sodium is linked to heart disease, obesity, strokes, and high blood pressure in adulthood.

2,300 mg
the maximum amount of sodium you should eat each day. That's about **1 teaspoon** and includes the salt that's already in some of the prepared foods you eat.

3,000 mg
how much sodium the average 9- to 13-year-old girl takes in

3,500 mg
how much sodium the average 9- to 13-year-old boy takes in

WHERE DOES ALL THAT SODIUM COME FROM?

It comes mostly from packaged foods and fast food. See how a few salty choices can really add up.

chicken noodle soup: 890 mg

pepperoni pizza: 880 mg

cheeseburger: 760 mg

mac and cheese: 570 mg

cheese pizza: 570 mg

hamburger: 540 mg

chicken nuggets (6 pieces): 500 mg

French fries (medium order): 430 mg

barbecue dipping sauce: 230 mg

ketchup: 100 mg

FAST-FOOD FACTS

• 34% of kids and teens eat fast food on any given day.

• 12% of teens get more than 40% of their daily calories from fast food.

Try not to sprinkle more salt on your already salty foods. You'll train your taste buds to want less salt — and your body will thank you.

SERVING SIZES . . . AND PORTIONS OUT OF CONTROL

Think the bag of chips you grab at the gas station is a single serving? How about candy at the movies? There may be more servings in that bag or box than you think. Check the label!

AVERAGE NUMBER OF SERVINGS

	0	1	2	3	4
package of cookies (2)					
bag of chips (3 oz.)					
movie theater candy (1 box)					

WHAT DOES A SERVING LOOK LIKE?

amount of chips in a serving

amount of chips in a snack bag

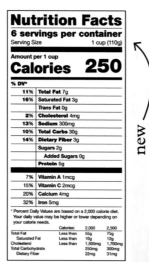

Nutrition Facts (old)
Serving Size 1 cup (110g)
Servings Per Container About 6

Amount Per Serving

Calories 250   Calories from Fat 30

	% Daily Value*
Total Fat 7g	**11%**
Saturated Fat 3g	**16%**
Trans Fat 0g	
Cholesterol 4mg	**2%**
Sodium 300mg	**13%**
Total Carbohydrate 30g	**10%**
Dietary Fiber 3g	**14%**
Sugars 2g	
Protein 5g	
Vitamin A	7%
Vitamin C	15%
Calcium	20%
Iron	32%

* Percent Daily Values are based on a 2,000 calorie diet. Your daily value may be higher or lower depending on your calorie needs.

	Calories:	2,000	2,500
Total Fat	Less than	55g	75g
Saturated Fat	Less than	10g	12g
Cholesterol	Less than	1,500mg	1,700mg
Total Carbohydrate		250mg	300mg
Dietary Fiber		22mg	31mg

Nutrition Facts (new)
6 servings per container
Serving Size   1 cup (110g)

Amount per 1 cup

Calories   250

% DV*

11%	**Total Fat** 7g	
16%	Saturated Fat 3g	
	Trans Fat 0g	
2%	**Cholesterol** 4mg	
13%	**Sodium** 300mg	
10%	**Total Carbs** 30g	
14%	**Dietary Fiber** 3g	
	Sugars 2g	
	Added Sugars 0g	
	Protein 5g	
7%	Vitamin A 1mcg	
15%	Vitamin C 2mcg	
20%	Calcium 4mcg	
32%	Iron 5mg	

* Percent Daily Values are based on a 2,000 calorie diet. Your daily value may be higher or lower depending on your calorie needs.

	Calories:	2,000	2,500
Total Fat	Less than	55g	75g
Saturated Fat	Less than	10g	12g
Cholesterol	Less than	1,500mg	1,700mg
Total Carbohydrate		250mg	300mg
Dietary Fiber		22mg	31mg

LABELS, OLD AND NEW

The Food and Drug Administration (FDA) is making it easier for you to figure out serving sizes and calories. Compare an old nutrition label to the new one, which was approved in 2016. See what's bigger and bolder?

20 minutes:

the time it takes your brain to know your stomach is full. If you eat a serving and still want more, wait before going back for seconds.

PORTIONS OVER TIME

A serving is the amount we should eat. But a portion is the amount we actually eat. Since the 1980s, portion sizes in restaurants, gas stations, and movie theaters have blown up — way up! See how they have changed in just 20 years.

Bagel

from this »» → to this

| 3 inches wide | 6 inches wide |
| 140 calories | 350 calories |

French fries

from this »» → to this

| 2.4 ounces | 6.9 ounces |
| 210 calories | 610 calories |

soda (regular, not diet)

from this »» → to this

| 6.5 ounces | 20 ounces |
| 85 calories | 250 calories |

movie popcorn

from this »» → to this

| 5 cups of popcorn | 11 cups of popcorn |
| 270 calories | 630 calories |

chocolate chip cookie

from this »» → to this

| 1.5 inches wide | 3.5 inches wide |
| 55 calories | 275 calories |

Just because you're given that much food doesn't mean you have to eat it all! Share with a friend, take half home, or stop eating as soon as you start feeling full.

Chapter 4

BODIES IN THE MEDIA

Do you ever compare your body to the models you see on TV or in magazines? Most girls do. But don't be fooled by what you see.

69%
of girls in 5th through 12th grade say that magazine pictures influence their idea of what a "perfect body" should look like.

48%
of girls wish they were as skinny as the models in fashion magazines.

WHAT'S REALISTIC?

Take a look at how a model's body compares to *most* women's bodies. And keep in mind that healthy bodies come in a wide variety of shapes and sizes.

the average woman in the U.S.

5' 4" tall
140 pounds

the average U.S. model

5' 11" tall
117 pounds

2%
the number of women who have a body like the ones shown in magazines

98%
the number of women who DON'T

DIGITAL MAGIC

Even most fashion models don't have the bodies you see in ads — their photographs are digitally edited to make them look perfect.

Want to change what you see in the media? You're not alone.

81% of girls would rather see true-to-life photos of models instead of touched-up, photo-edited ones.

So speak up and say so! Email or write to your favorite magazines and tell them to show *real* women and girls — like you.

BODY IMAGE

As your body changes, so does the way you see yourself in the mirror and in your mind. Many girls have a negative body image during their tween and teen years. Here are the numbers — and how to turn them around.

More than **80%** of 10-year-olds are afraid of being fat.

Age 10

20: the age when self-esteem starts to improve for most girls

Age 20

Age 6

A girl's unhappiness with her body can start as early as **age 6**.

Age 12-15

Between the ages of **12 and 15**, when most girls have entered puberty, their satisfaction with their bodies is at an all-time low.

About **31%** of children and teens are overweight or obese.

DANGERS OF DIETING

68% of 15-year-old girls are on a diet.

8% of those are on a severe or unhealthy diet.

Adolescent girls who diet are 5 times more likely to develop an eating disorder.

But there are healthy ways to manage your weight. Talk to your parents or your doctor for a nutrition plan that will help you — not hurt you.

WHAT GIVES BODY IMAGE A BOOST?

Playing sports and exercise.

 Girls **ages 9 to 11** who play sports report higher self-esteem even **2 years** later.

 Middle-school girls who play at least **3 sports** a year have a healthier body image than girls who don't.

53% of teens say they feel good about themselves after exercising.

Chapter 5

WORKING IT OUT

Why exercise? Not only does it burn calories to keep your body at a healthy weight, but it makes you feel good too.

THE MORE ACTIVE YOU ARE, THE MORE CALORIES YOU NEED.

See for yourself. An active 9-year-old needs just as many calories every day as an idle 14-year-old.

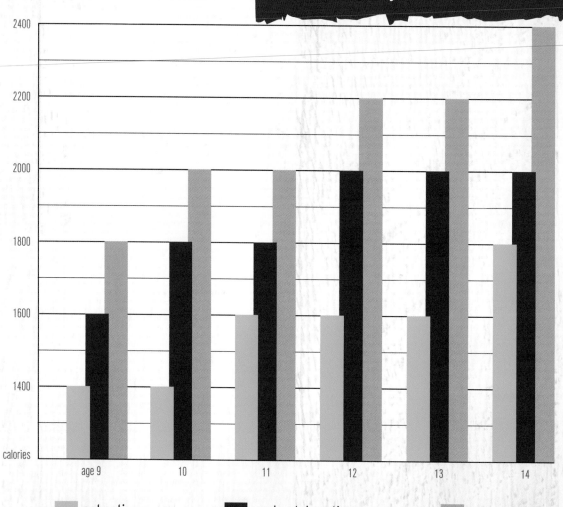

not active | moderately active | very active

GIRLS VS. BOYS

When it comes to exercise, experts recommend that kids and adolescents get at least 60 minutes a day. But most aren't getting enough.

30 to 33%

of boys between ages 11 and 15 in the U.S. are getting enough physical activity. But only . . .

24%

of 11-year-old girls get enough exercise each day.

And by age 15, that percentage drops to

17%.

WANT TO GET MORE EXERCISE?

Check this list for ideas — and the number of girls in grades 3 through 12 who took part in each activity last year.

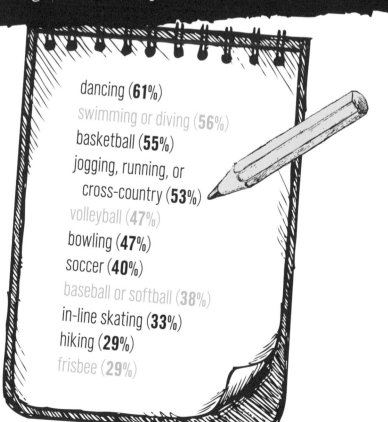

dancing (**61%**)
swimming or diving (**56%**)
basketball (**55%**)
jogging, running, or cross-country (**53%**)
volleyball (**47%**)
bowling (**47%**)
soccer (**40%**)
baseball or softball (**38%**)
in-line skating (**33%**)
hiking (**29%**)
frisbee (**29%**)

WORKOUT REMINDERS

- Don't eat within 1 hour before your workout. You might get cramps or feel sick.

- Drink water every 15 to 20 minutes while you work out, especially during hot weather. But don't chug it! Take slow sips.

SPORTS STATS

Organized sports are a great way to get the exercise you need.
The benefits go way beyond strengthening your body.

69% of middle- and high-school girls and
73% of boys play at least one sport.
Many play more than one.

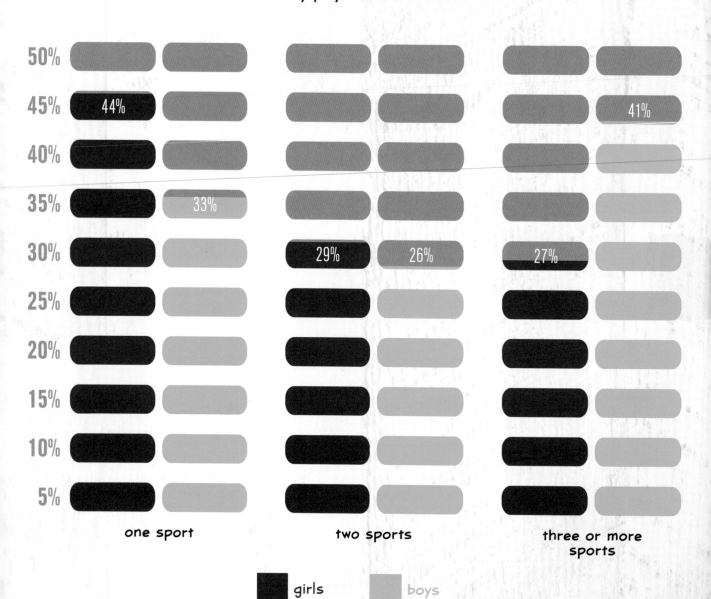

| | 50% | 45% | 40% | 35% | 30% | 25% | 20% | 15% | 10% | 5% |

one sport — girls 44%, boys 33%
two sports — girls 29%, boys 26%
three or more sports — girls 27%, boys 41%

girls   boys

THE BIG 3

Which sports are most popular
among middle-school girls?

61%
of girls dance.

59%
play volleyball.

46%
play soccer.

5 REASONS TO PLAY SPORTS
Some of the benefits might surprise you!

Girls who take part in sports . . .

1 watch less TV

2 get better grades

3 are less depressed

4 are less likely to smoke

5 stay at a healthier weight

. . . than girls who don't.

TIME OUT
It's OK to give your body a break. Experts recommend that
you work out no more than **5 days** a week and take time
off from each sport at least **2 to 3 months** a year.

Chapter 6

TREAT YOUR BODY RIGHT

If you're as busy as most girls your age, you might grab a soda or an energy drink to keep going. But beware. Too much caffeine can make you feel jittery, anxious, or dizzy. It can also keep you up at night, which will make you feel even more tired tomorrow.

100 mg
is the maximum amount of caffeine adolescents and teens should consume in any one day.

500 mg
is how much caffeine some energy drinks have! Make sure to check the label to see how many servings are inside.

100 mg a day
is enough to make you dependent on caffeine. That means you might get headaches or feel tired or cranky when you quit drinking it.

68%
of adolescents consume energy drinks.

6 hours
is how long after drinking caffeine that you might still feel its effects.

85%
of U.S. parents want warning labels placed on energy drinks.

STILL WANT CAFFEINE?

Choose a drink with a lower level so that you don't take in more than 100 mg a day and can still sleep at night.

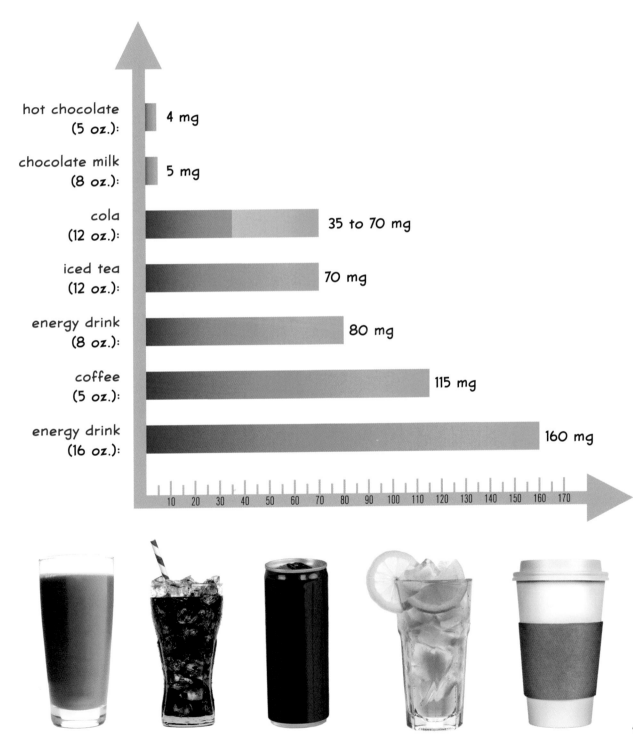

hot chocolate (5 oz.): 4 mg

chocolate milk (8 oz.): 5 mg

cola (12 oz.): 35 to 70 mg

iced tea (12 oz.): 70 mg

energy drink (8 oz.): 80 mg

coffee (5 oz.): 115 mg

energy drink (16 oz.): 160 mg

10 20 30 40 50 60 70 80 90 100 110 120 130 140 150 160 170

CIGARETTES, DRUGS, AND ALCOHOL

Kids your age are getting smart about substance abuse and experimenting less with cigarettes, drugs, and alcohol. Who still uses these dangerous substances and why?

STATS ON SMOKING

2%
middle-school students who smoke regular (tobacco) cigarettes

480,000:
the number of people who die each year from smoking tobacco

9%
high-school students who smoke regular cigarettes

THE GOOD NEWS?

Most kids aren't smoking every day, and a lot fewer kids are doing it today than 20 years ago. See for yourself:

8th graders in 1996 — **10%** smoked daily.

10th graders in 1996 — **18%** smoked daily.

8th graders in 2016 — **1%** smoked daily.

10th graders in 2016 — **2%** smoked daily.

These pen-like devices deliver nicotine through vapor instead of smoke. Vaping may seem safer because the vapor comes in different flavors and doesn't involve burning tobacco. But e-cigarettes still contain nicotine, which is very addictive.

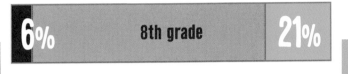

used e-cigarettes in 2016

6% 8th grade **21%**

10% 10th grade **19%**

view repeated use of e-cigarettes as harmful

81% of users said they used e-cigarettes because of the appealing flavors. But . . .

If you try e-cigarettes by the time you start 9th grade, you may be more likely to start smoking regular cigarettes **within the next year.**

ALCOHOL AND OTHER DRUGS

THE GOOD NEWS:

-Fewer adolescents drink alcohol and smoke marijuana today than **5** years ago.

-Use of other illegal drugs is at its lowest rate in the past **20** years!

Who used alcohol, marijuana, and other illegal drugs in 2016?

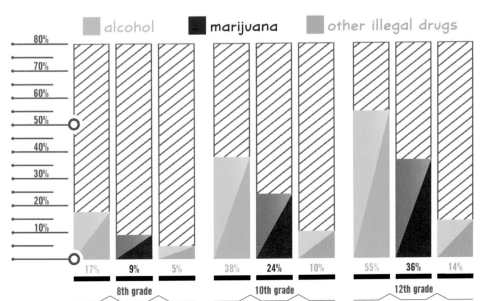

alcohol   marijuana   other illegal drugs

	8th grade			10th grade			12th grade	
17%	9%	5%	38%	24%	10%	55%	36%	14%

GETTING YOUR ZZZS

Sleep is like food for your body and brain. But many kids and teens aren't getting enough. Experts recommend at least **10 hours** a night for children and **9 to 10 hours** for teens. See who's getting their zzzs — and who isn't.

WHO GETS AT LEAST 9 HOURS A NIGHT?

The older you get, the more difficult it is to get the sleep you need. Why? During adolescence, your sleep patterns shift. Your body wants to stay awake longer at night and sleep in later in the morning.

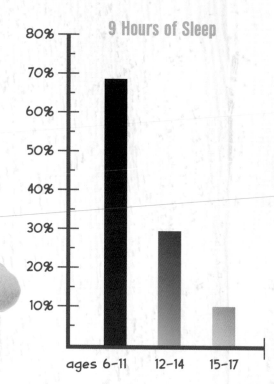

9 Hours of Sleep

WHAT ELSE GETS IN THE WAY?

Lots of things interfere with a good night's sleep, but busy schedules and homework top the list. Here are the numbers of kids and teens who can't sleep due to . . .

1. evening activities: **34%**

2. homework: **28%**

3. the temperature of the room (too hot or too cold): **18%**

4. noise in the house: **15%**

5. pets: **9%**

ELECTRONIC DEVICES? TURN 'EM OFF!

Leaving on devices like your TV, tablet, or phone can interfere with sleep.

get a good night's sleep

45% of kids who turn off their devices

25% of kids who leave them on

wake up at night

41% of kids who turn them off

52% of kids who leave them on

sometimes fall asleep at school

16% of kids who turn them off

36% of kids who leave them on

1 more hour

That's how much extra sleep kids and teens get each night if their parents enforce rules about bedtime.
Try to follow them — that extra hour is worth it!

3 WAYS TO UNWIND BEFORE BED

1. 30% of kids take a bath or shower.

2. 24% listen to music.

3. 21% read.

Your body and mind have a strong connection. If you explore the ways your body and mind work together, you'll feel more in control of both, especially as you head into your teen years.

STRESSED OUT!

31%

of teens ages **13 to 17** say they feel more stressed than they did **a year ago.** And because of that stress . . .

40%

of kids report that they worry too much.

36% feel more tired than usual.

30% of teens feel depressed or sad.

23% sometimes skip meals.

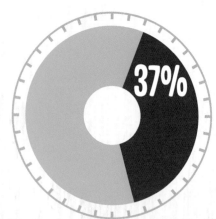

37%

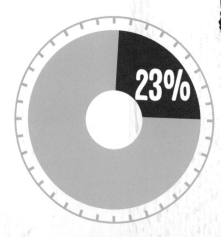

23%

GIRLS VS. BOYS

37% of teen girls report feeling sad or depressed in the past month because of stress. Compare that to 23% of teen boys.

HOW DO TWEENS AND TEENS MANAGE STRESS?

■ tweens (ages 8 to 12)   ■ teens (ages 13 to 17)

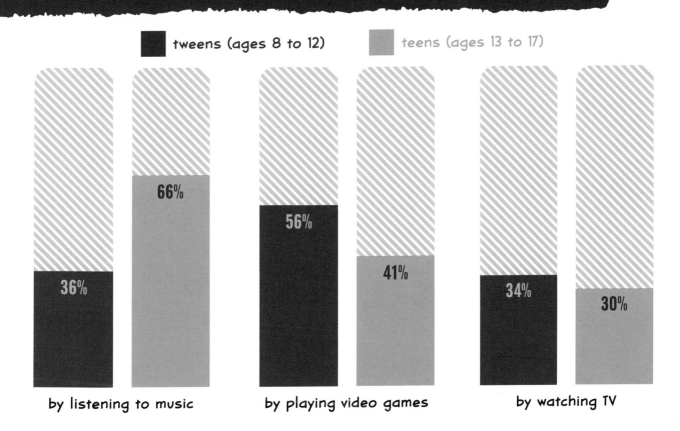

36%	66%	
	56%	
	41%	34%	30%

by listening to music   by playing video games   by watching TV

WHAT ELSE HELPS?

MOVING YOUR BODY!

After exercising . . .

- **53%** of teens say they feel good about themselves.
- **40%** say they're in a good mood.
- **32%** say they feel less stressed.

| 53% | 40% | 32% |

HITTING THE SHEETS

1 in 5
teens say that when they don't get enough sleep, they're more stressed.

BODY TALK

Who do girls talk to when they're feeling stressed or have questions about their bodies? Most talk to friends or other girls their own age. Some talk to their parents, especially their moms. Others talk to a teacher, an aunt, or another adult they trust.

83%
83% of teens say they have someone who is about their same age that they trust and can confide in, such as a friend, sister, or cousin.

15%
15% say they don't have someone like that in their lives.

78%
78% of teens say there's an adult other than a parent whom they can trust and confide in, such as a teacher, coach, family friend, or aunt.

21%
21% say they don't have another adult they confide in.

9th–12th grade
9th to 12th grade girls confide more in their parents than boys do – especially in their moms.

83%
83% of teen girls said they write down their problems in a journal or diary.

6 TIPS FOR TALKING TO ADULTS

Being a teenager is exciting and sometimes confusing. It's easier to get through the confusing times if you have a trusted adult to talk to — someone who's been through what you're going through. But it's not always easy to feel comfortable talking to adult. These tips might make it easier.

1. **Start with small talk.** The more you practice talking – even about the small, silly stuff – the easier it'll be to talk about the big stuff.

2. **Pick the right time.** Make sure you have enough time to actually talk. Talk to a teacher after school instead of before. Talk to a parent while riding in the car.

3. **Say what you need.** Just someone to hear you out? Or do you want advice? Be specific.

4. **Say what you feel.** If you're scared to talk about what's been going on with you or you are embarrassed to ask a question, say so!

5. **Take a break** if things get too heated. Come back to the conversation later, when you're feeling more calm.

6. **Keep talking.** The more you do, the easier it'll get. You'll figure out your feelings, find answers to questions, and feel more in control of your life – and your changing body.

Author Bio

Erin Falligant has written more than 30 fiction and nonfiction books for children. Her advice books help tweens stand up to bullies, survive homework, and embrace their changing bodies. Erin earned an M.S. in Child Clinical Psychology and worked for more than 15 years as a children's book editor. She stays in touch with girls as a volunteer for Girls on the Run in her hometown of Madison, Wisconsin.

Books in This Set

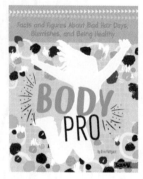

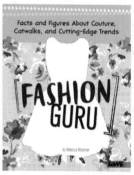